This book belongs to :

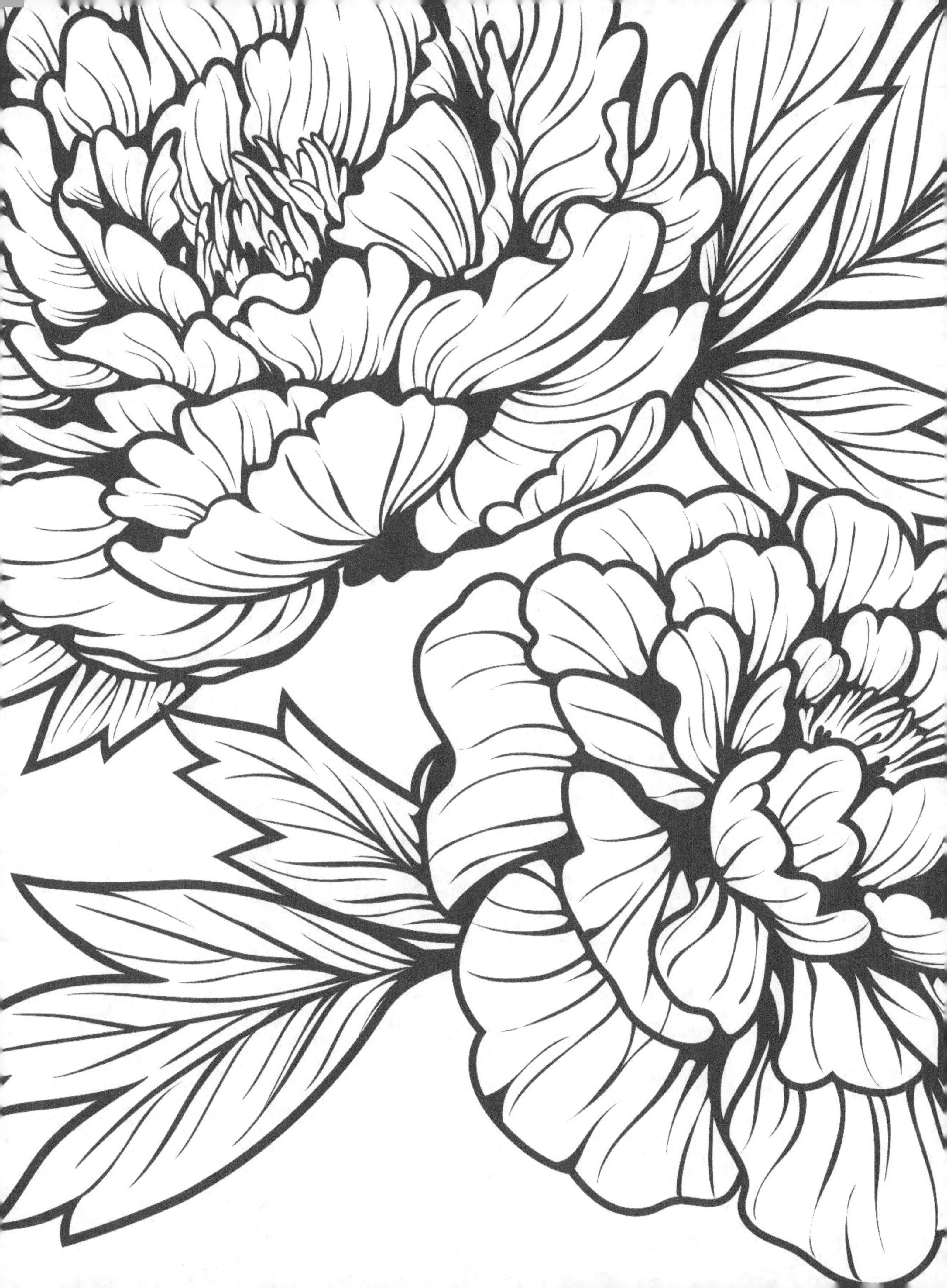

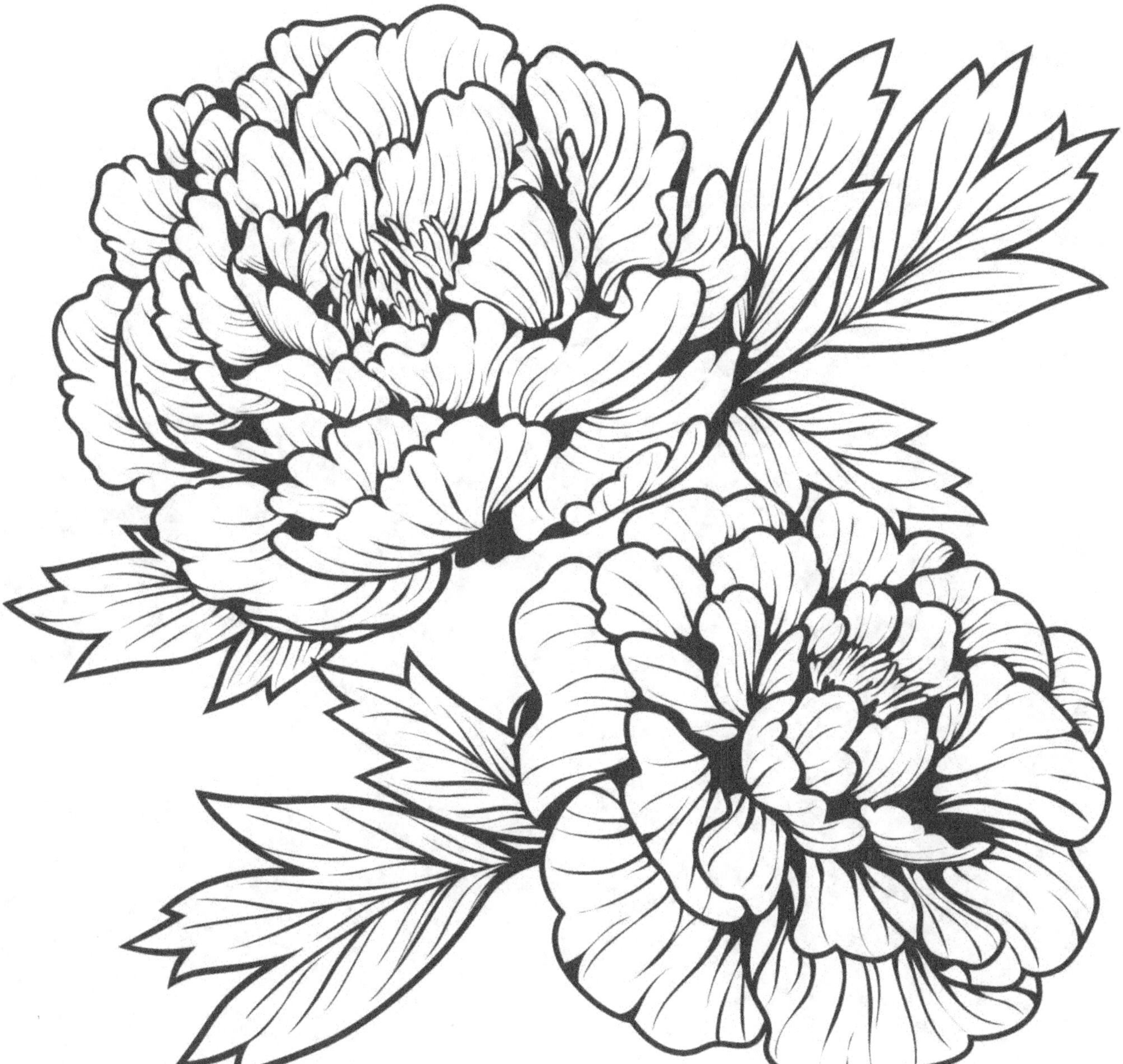

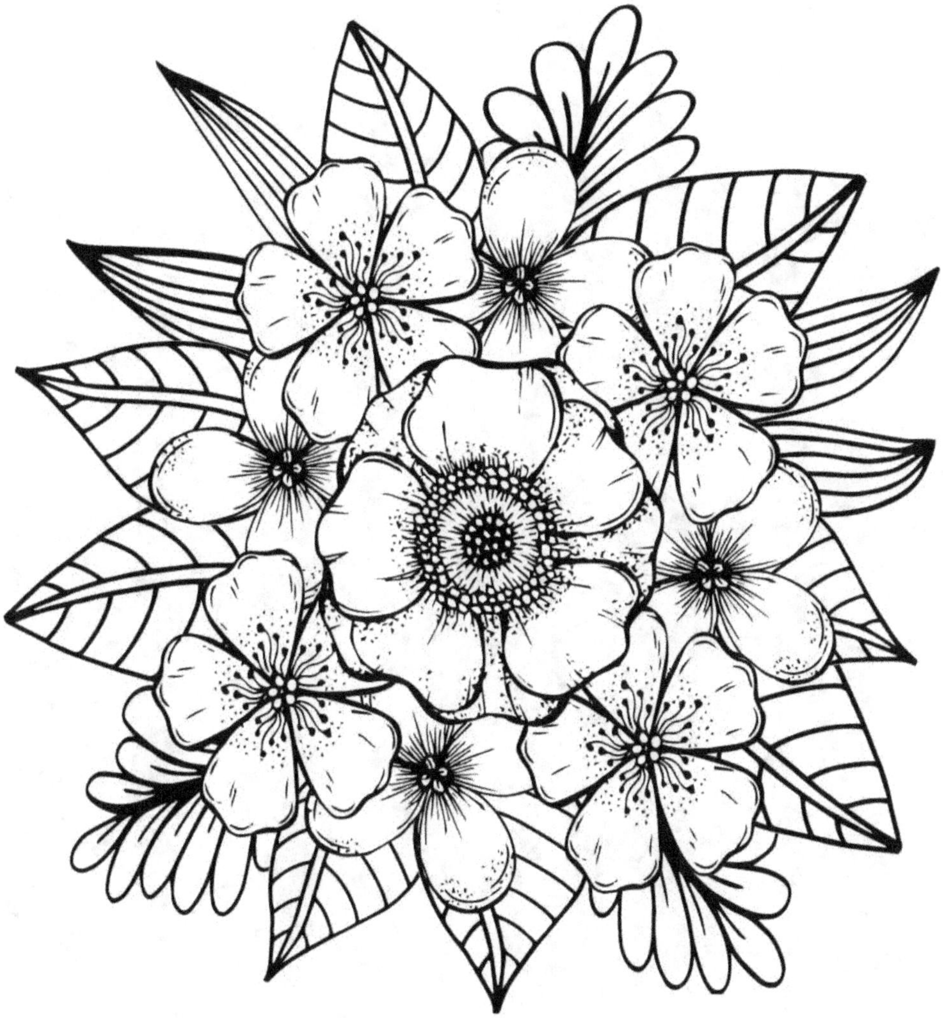

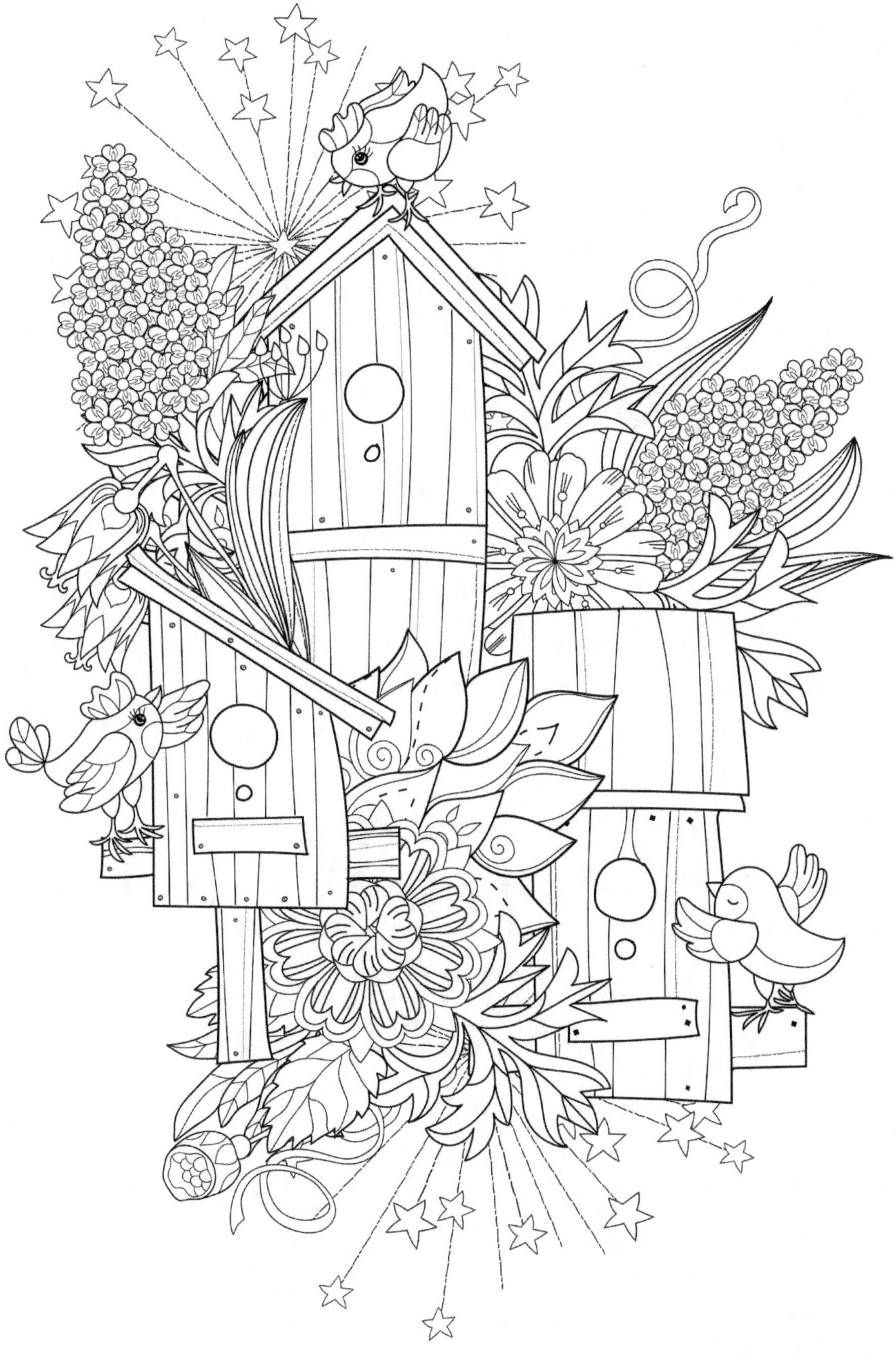

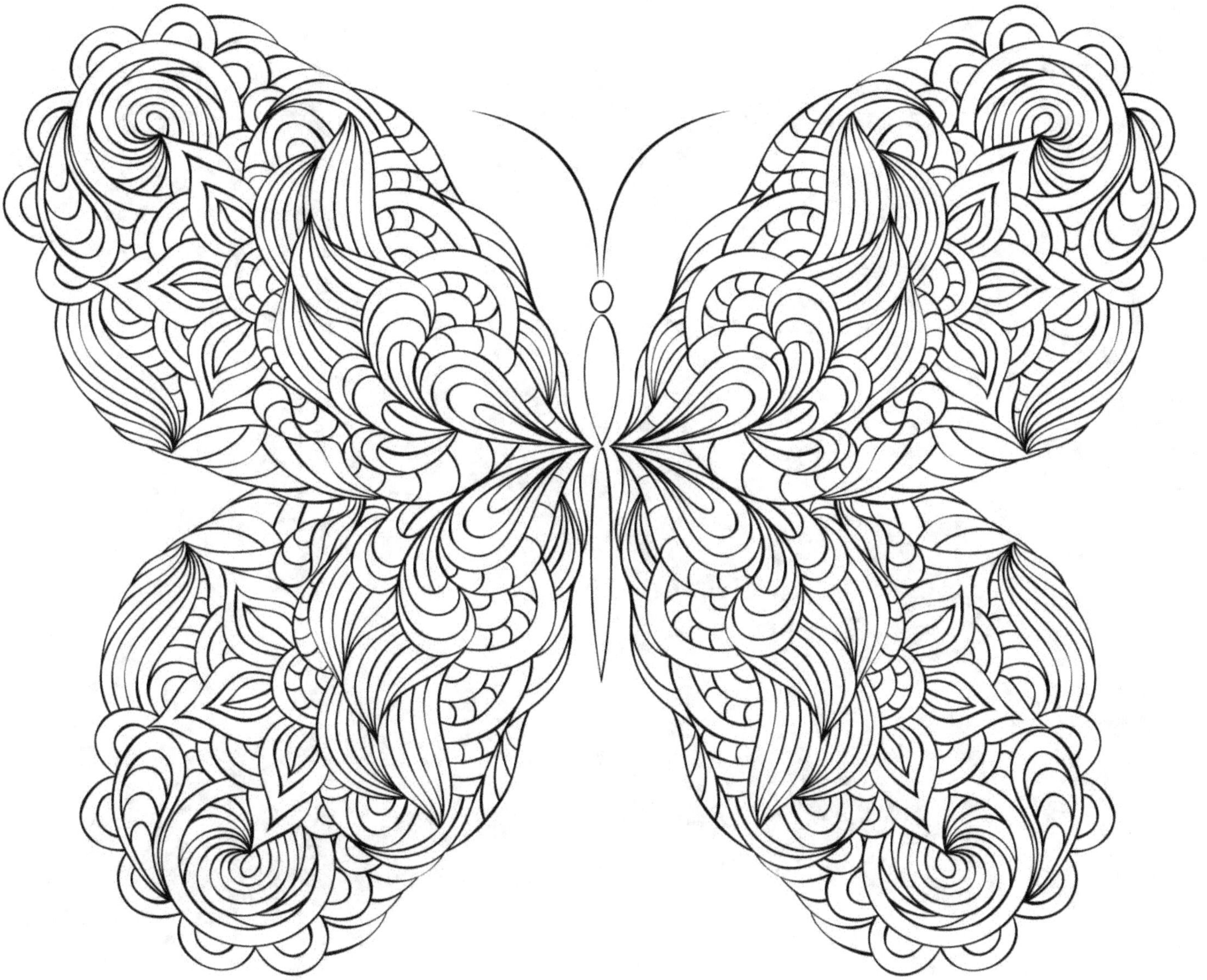

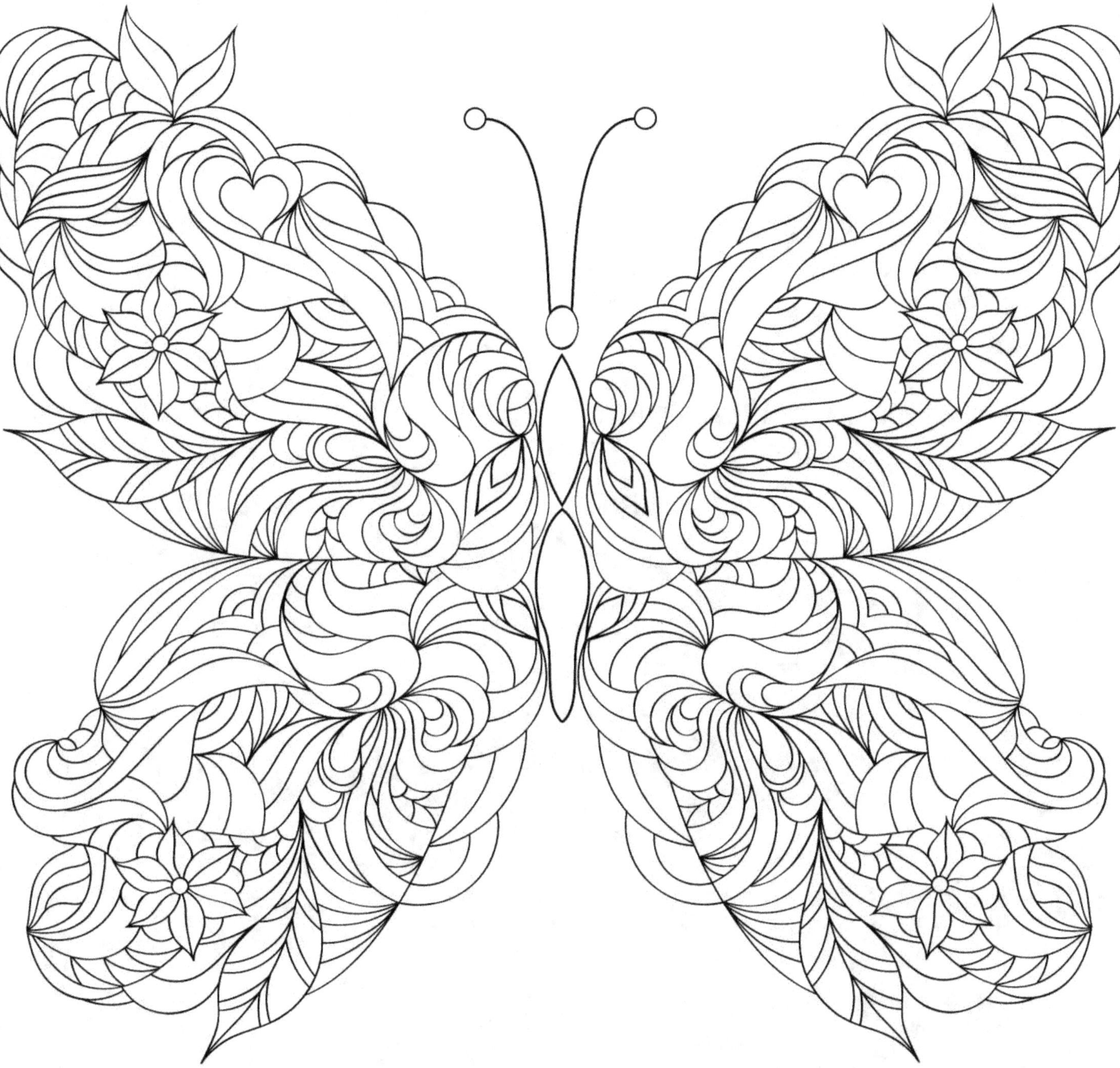

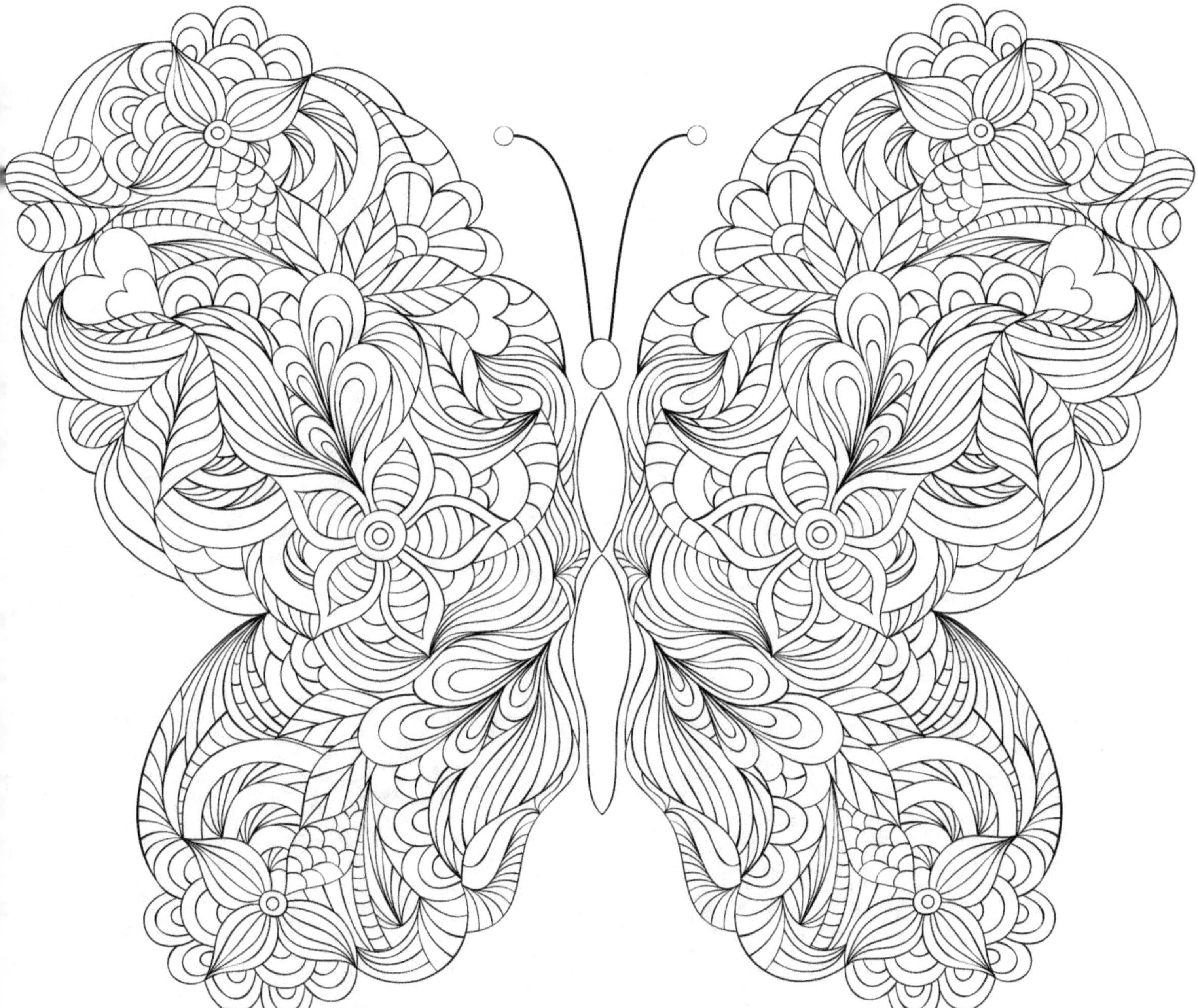

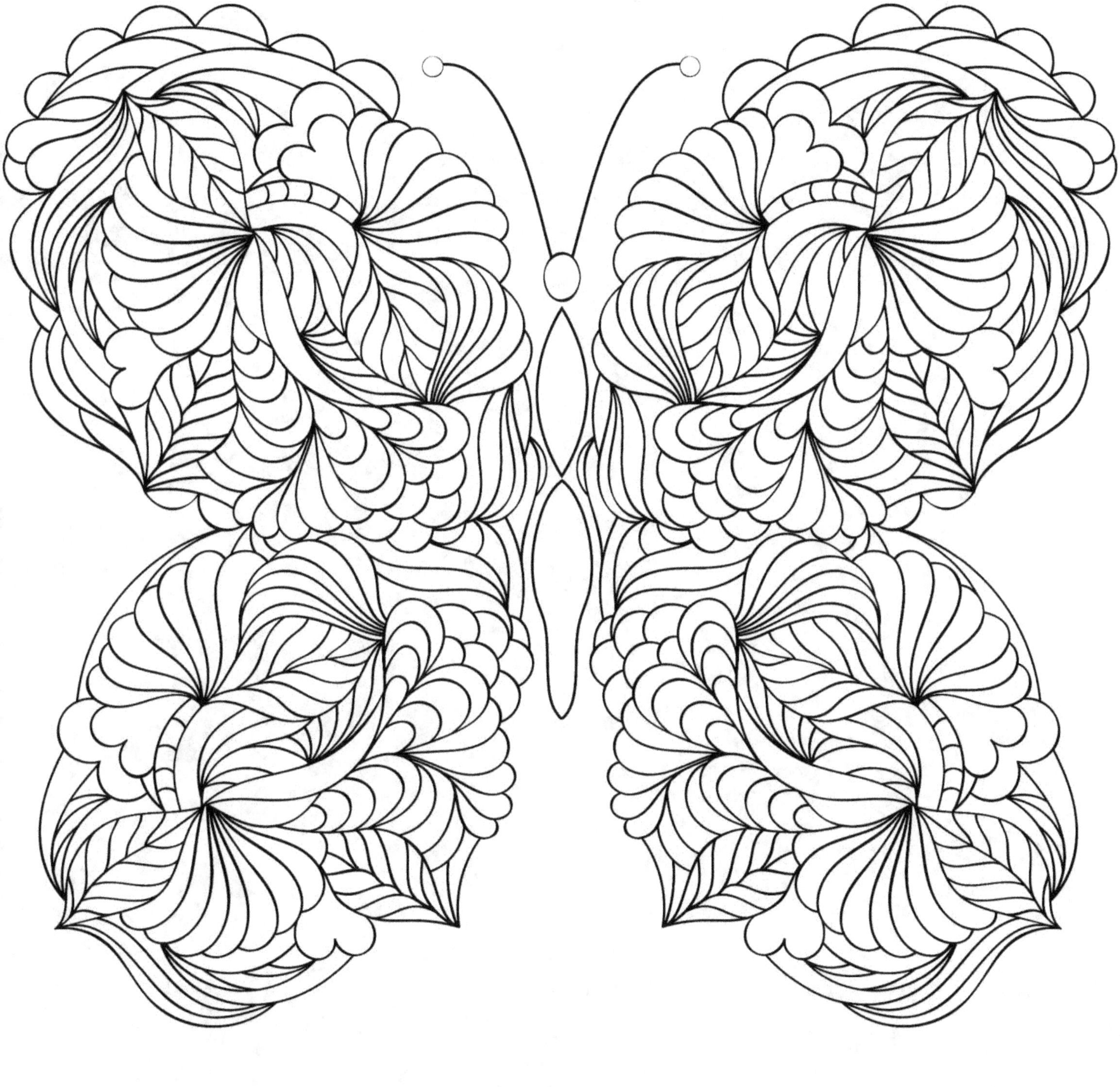

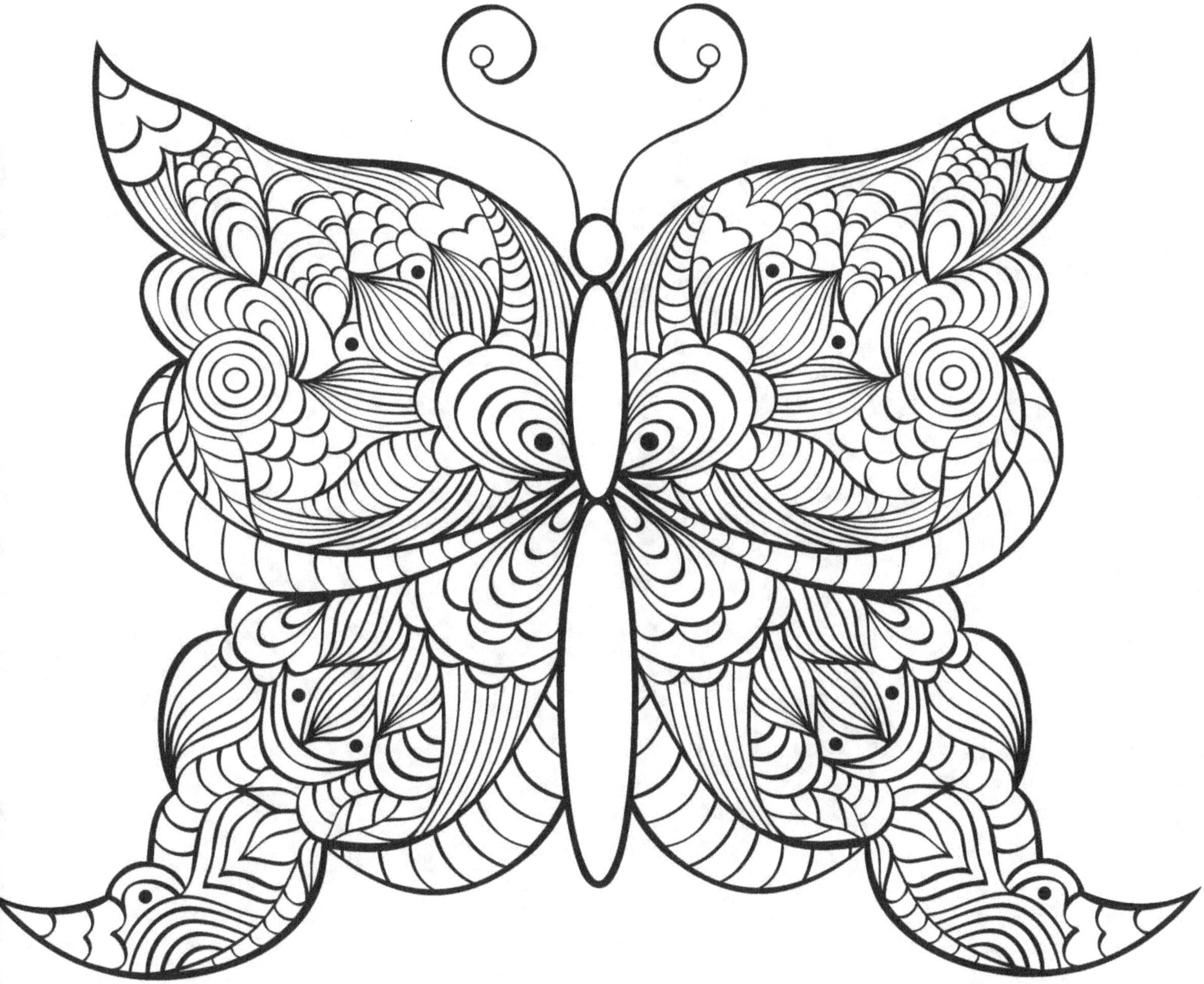

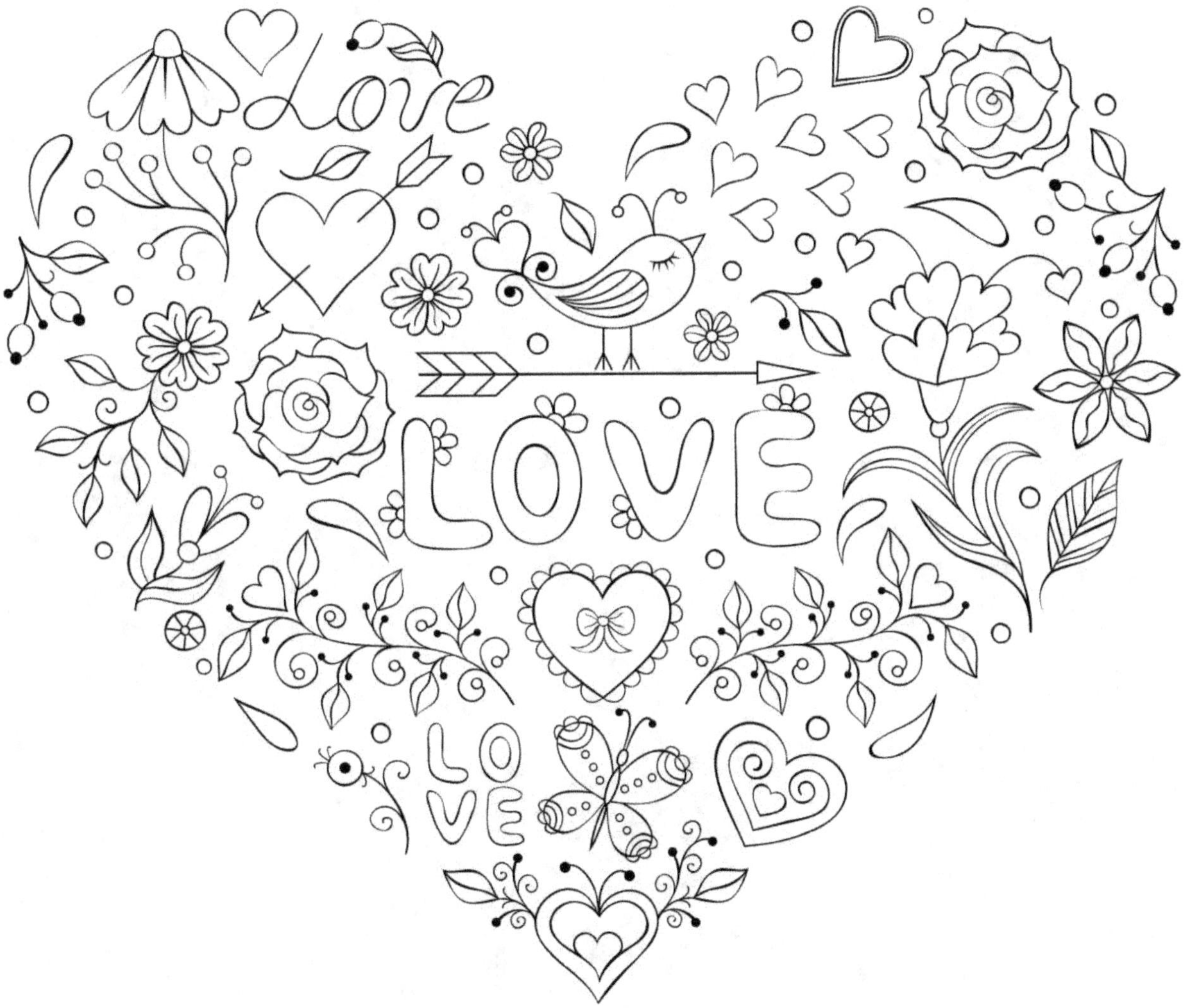
Love
LOVE
LO
VE

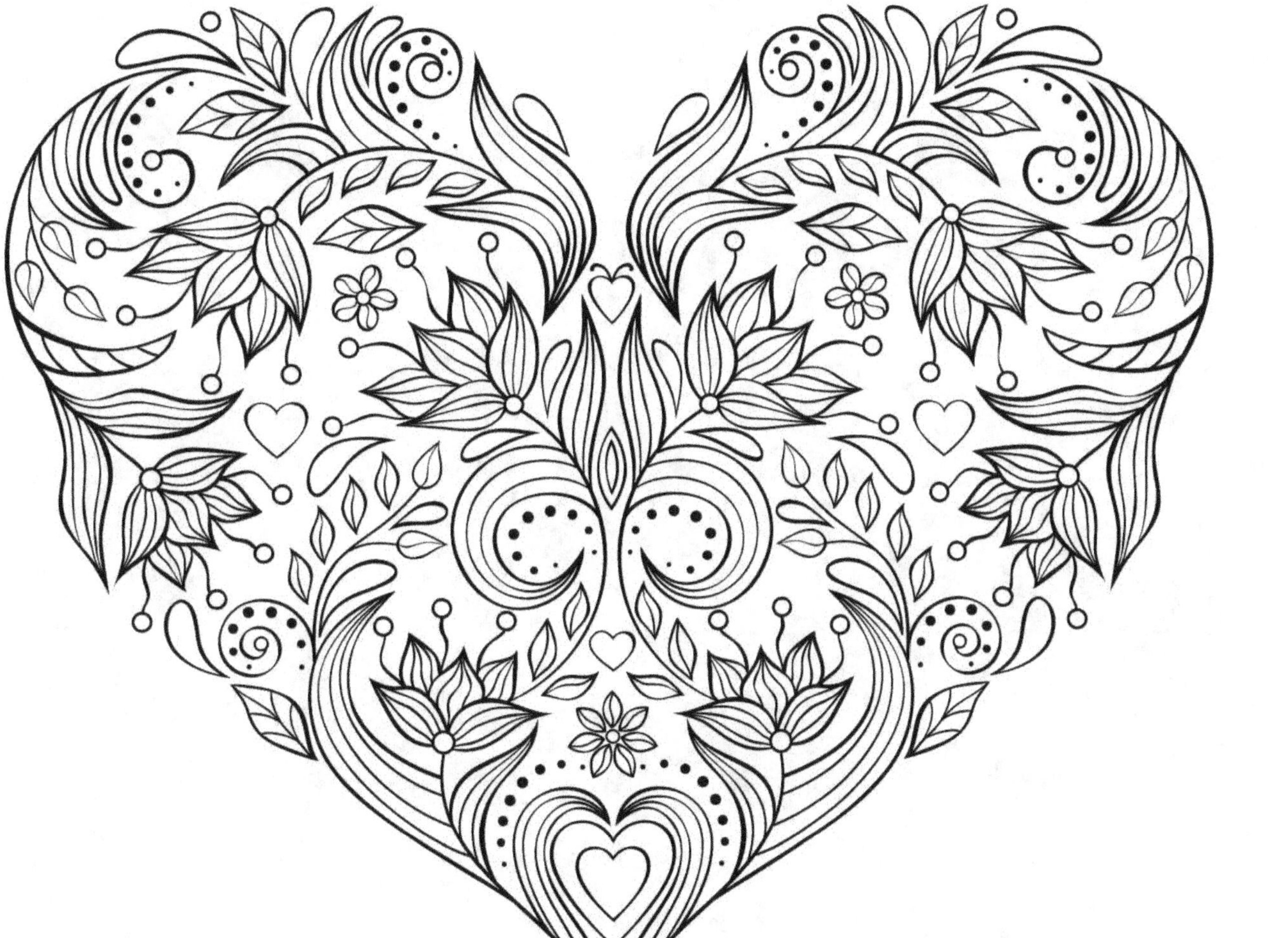

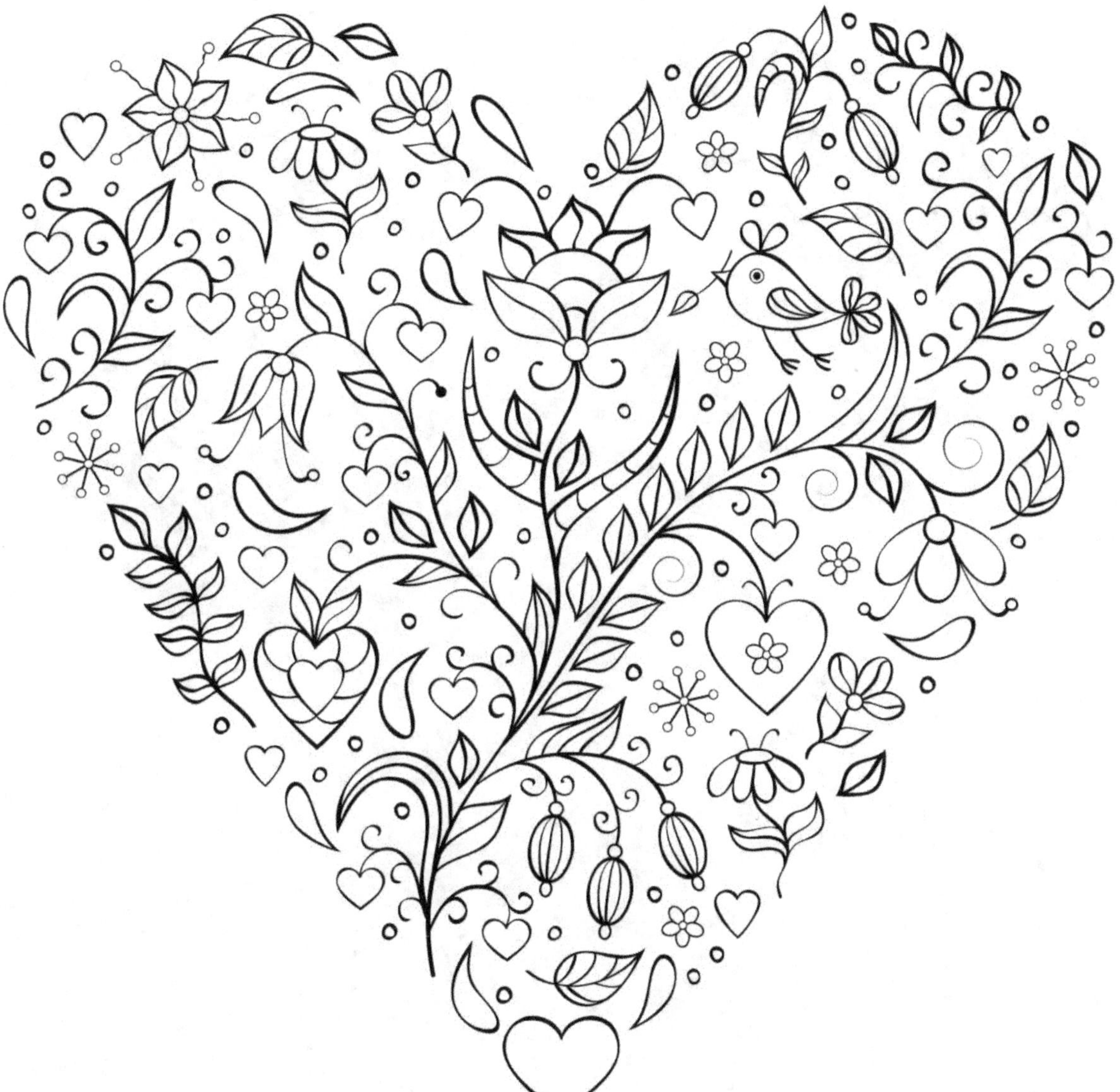

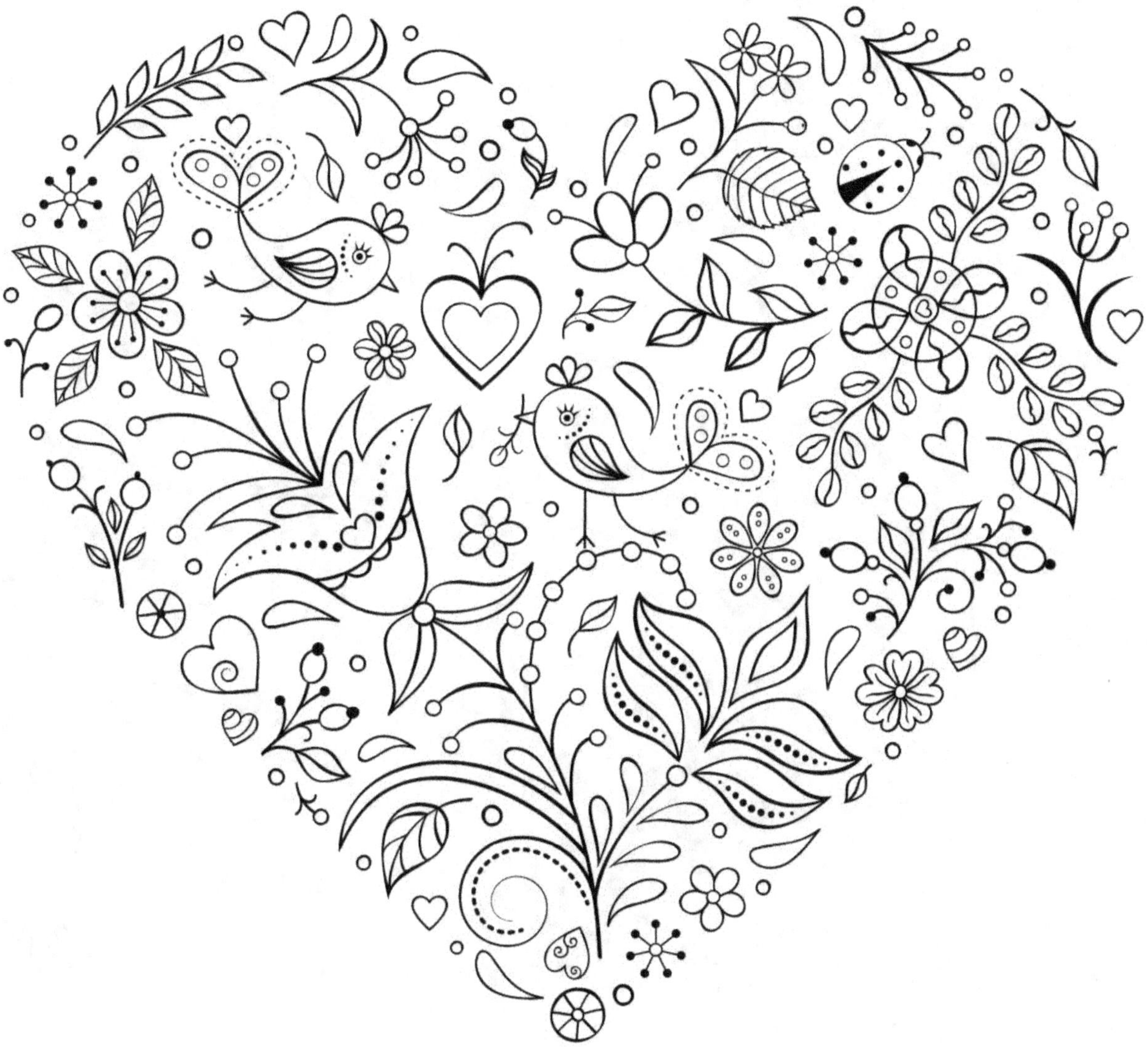

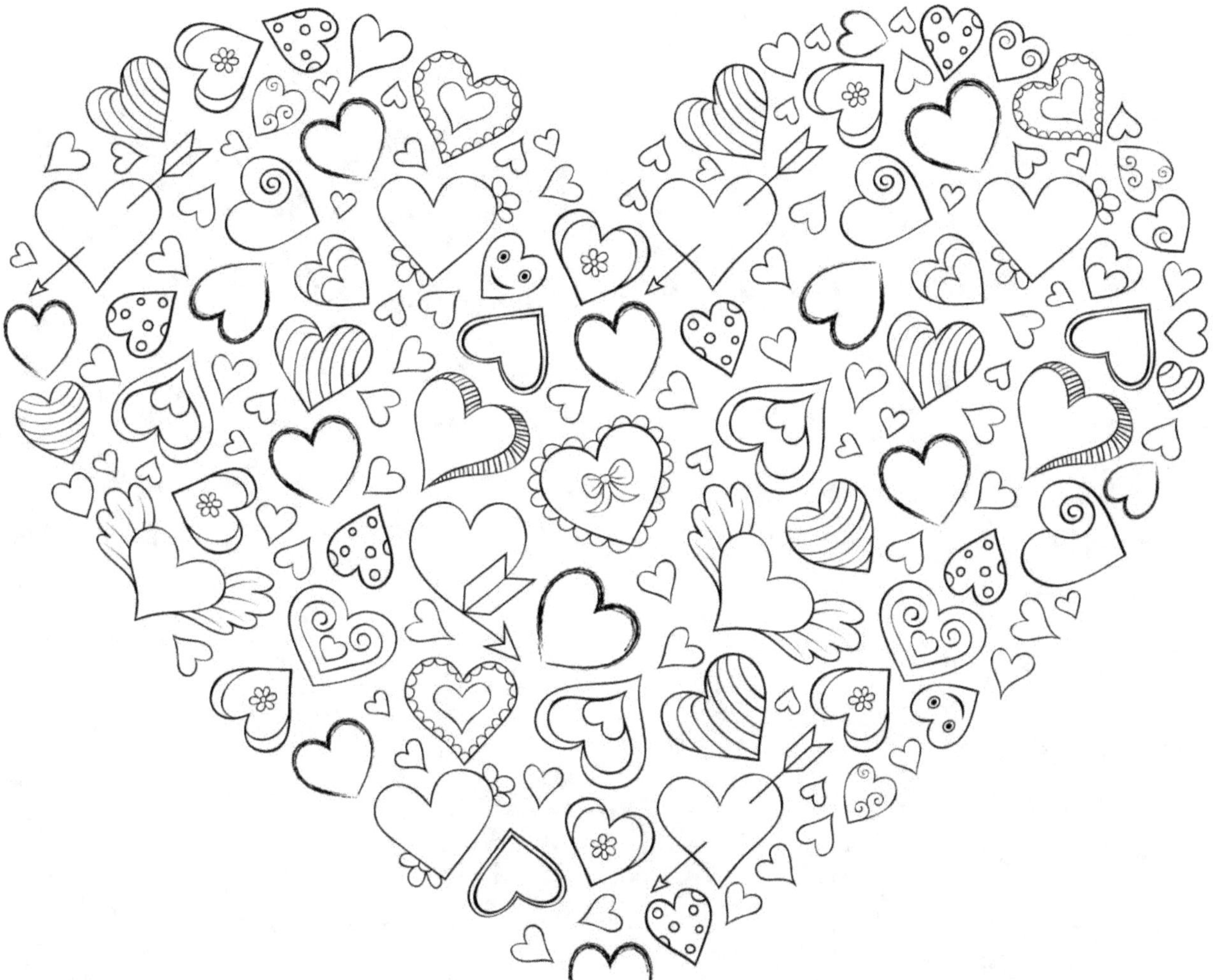

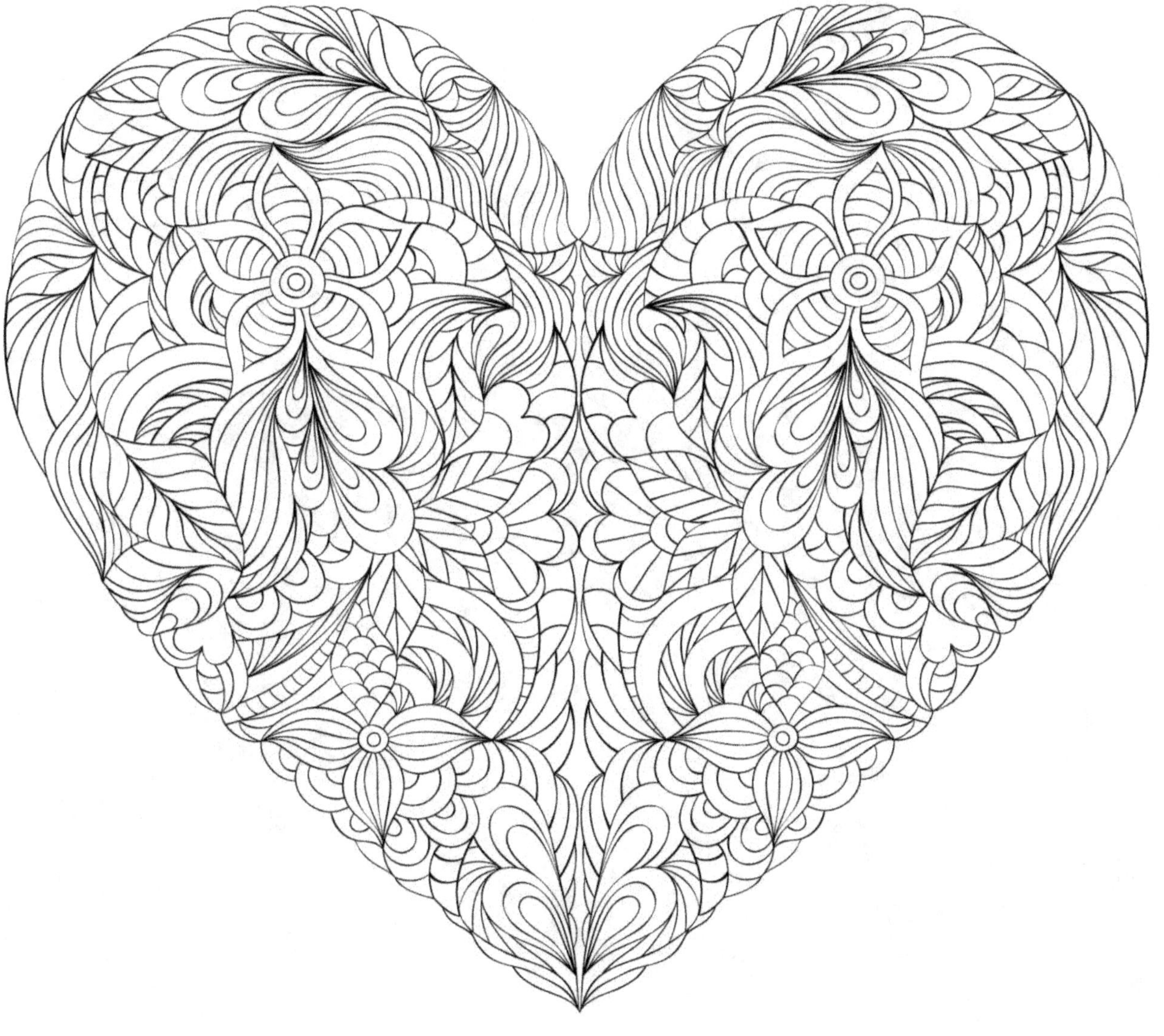

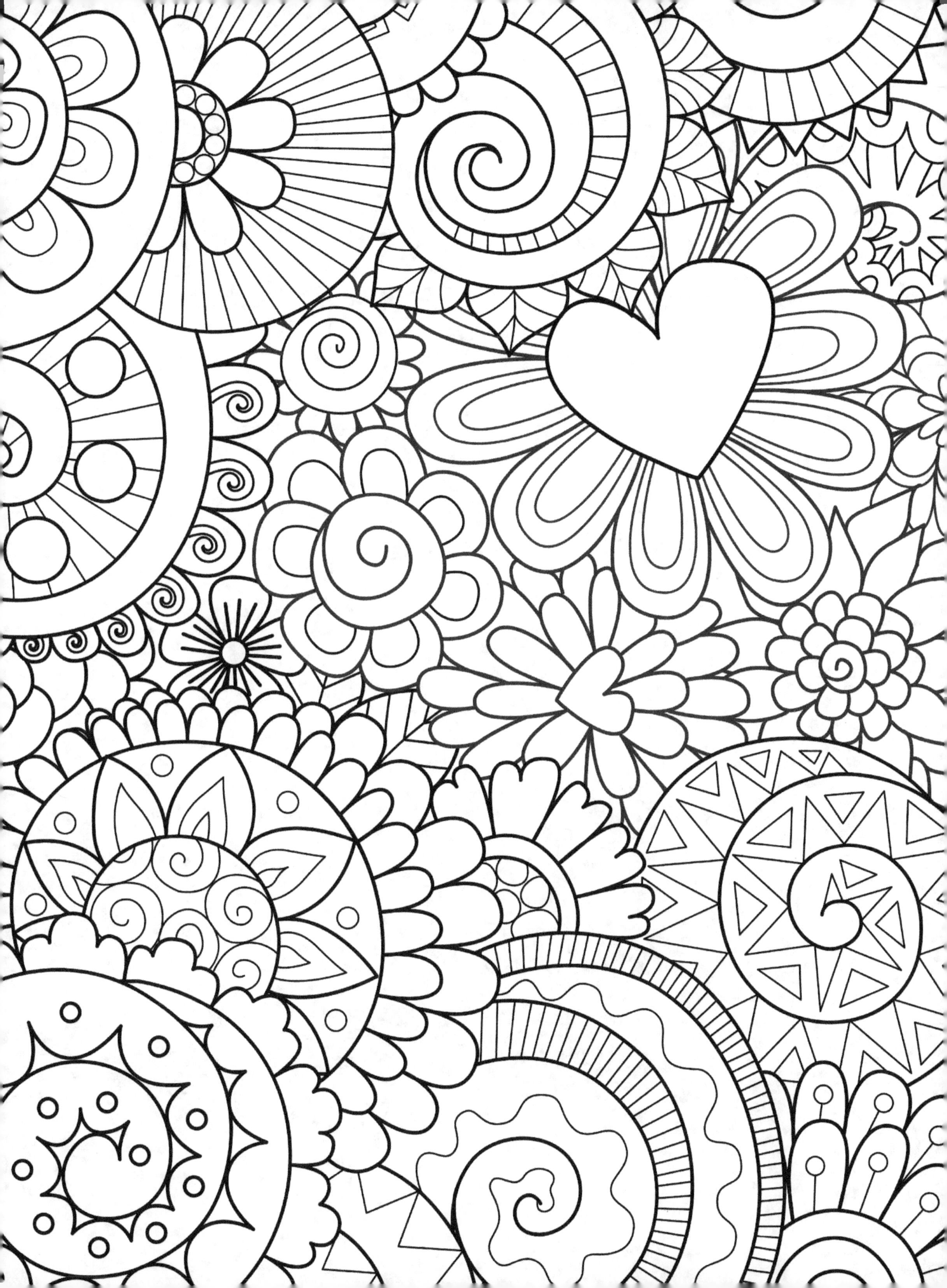

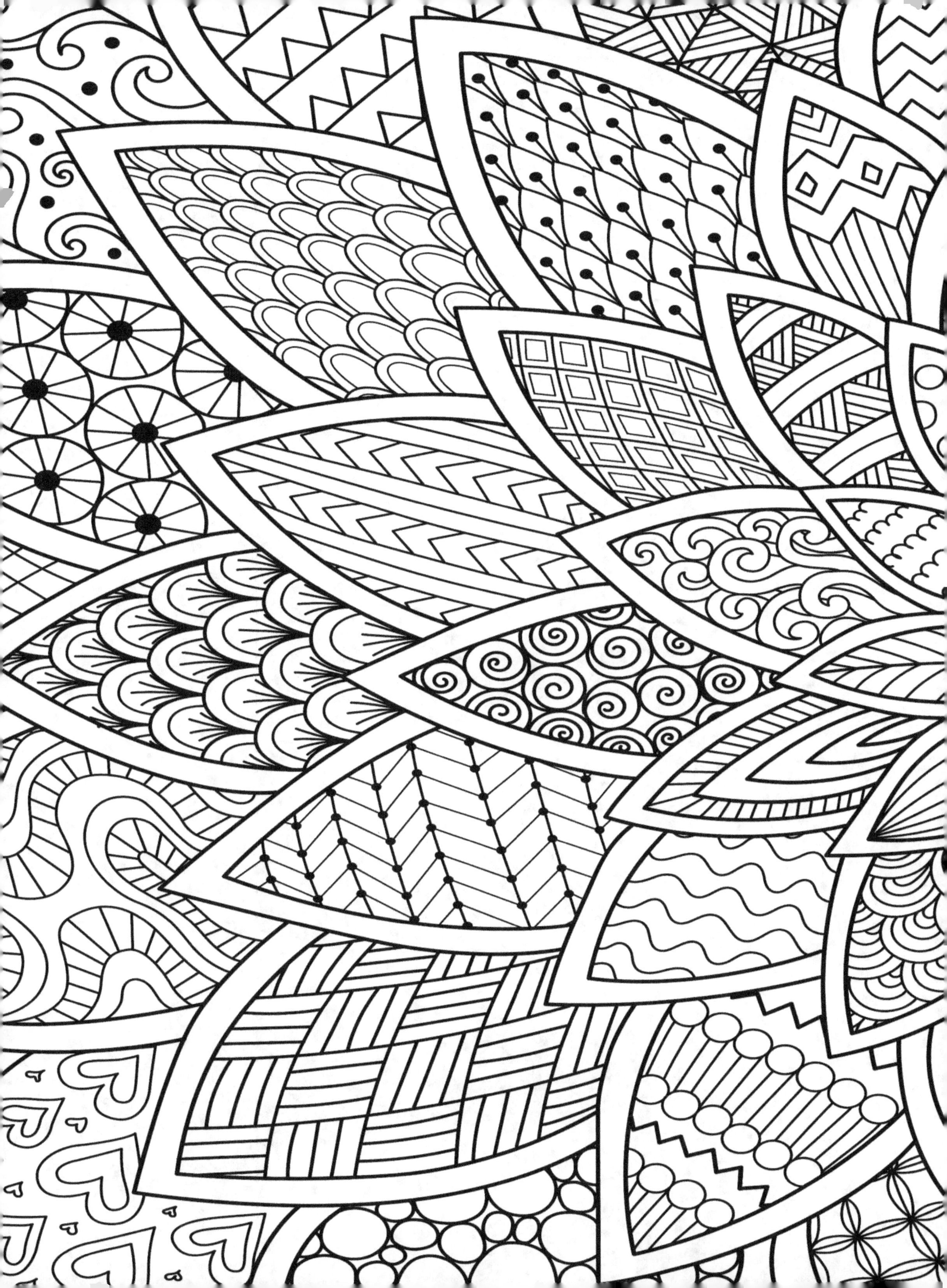

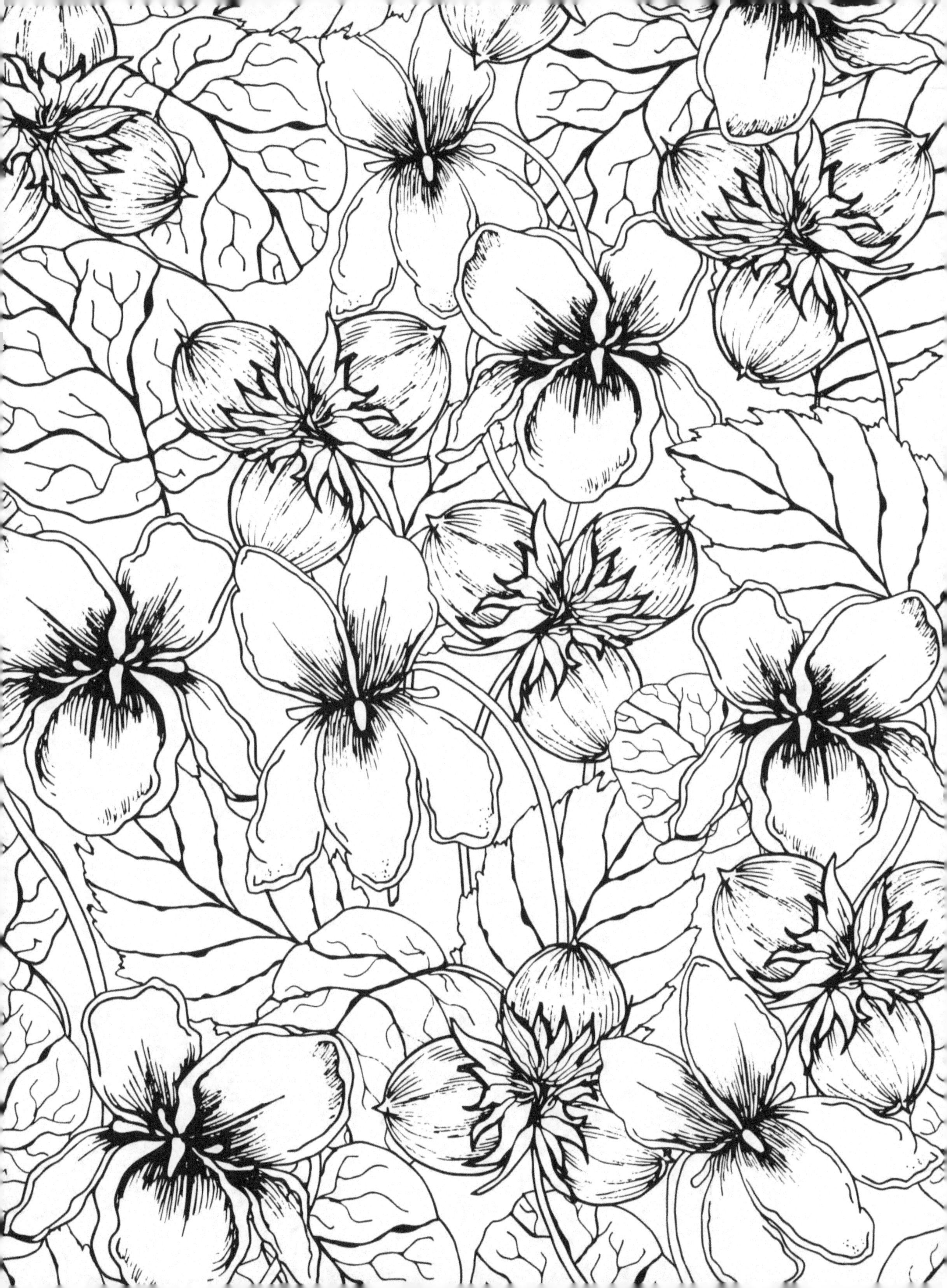

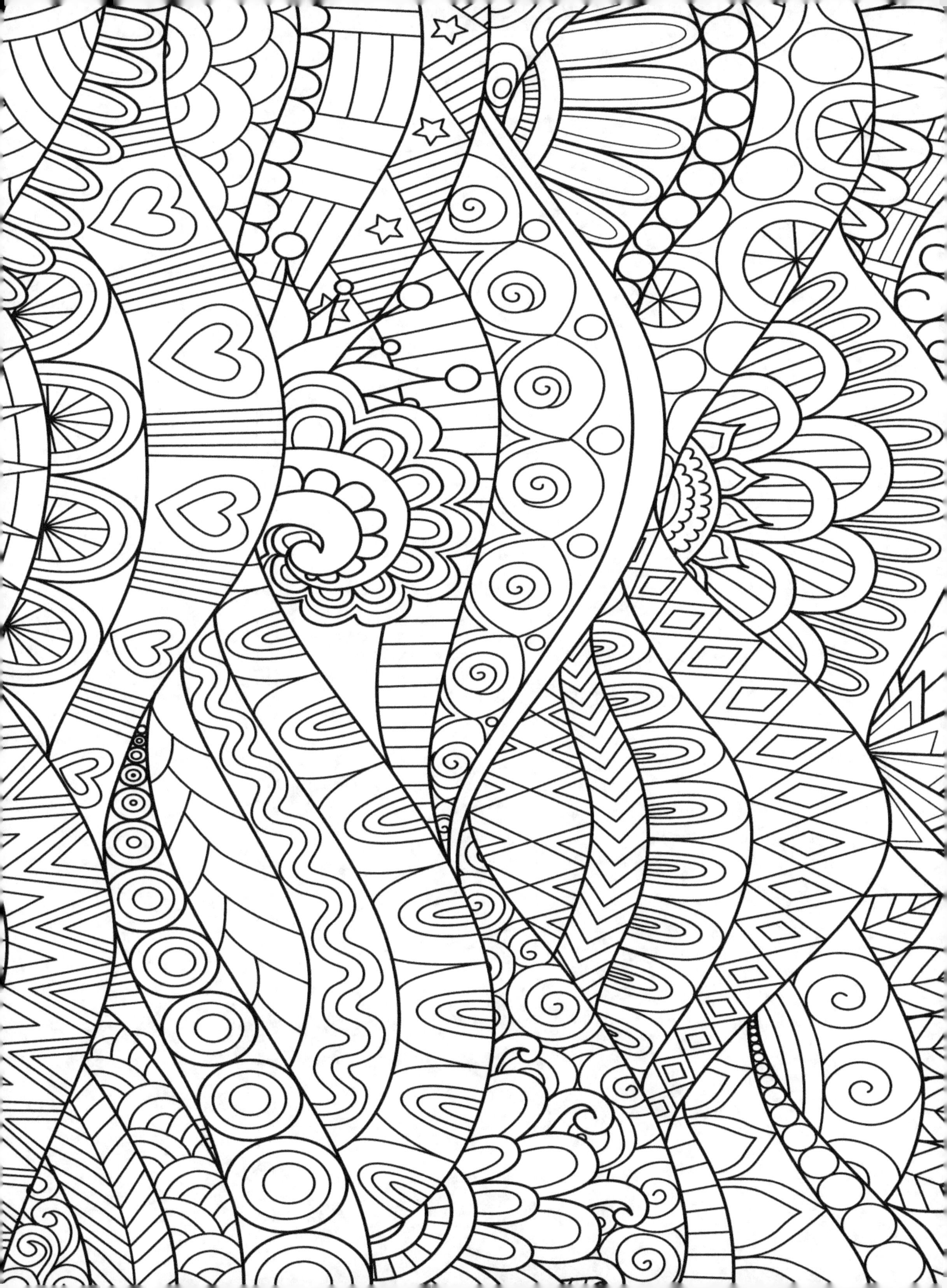

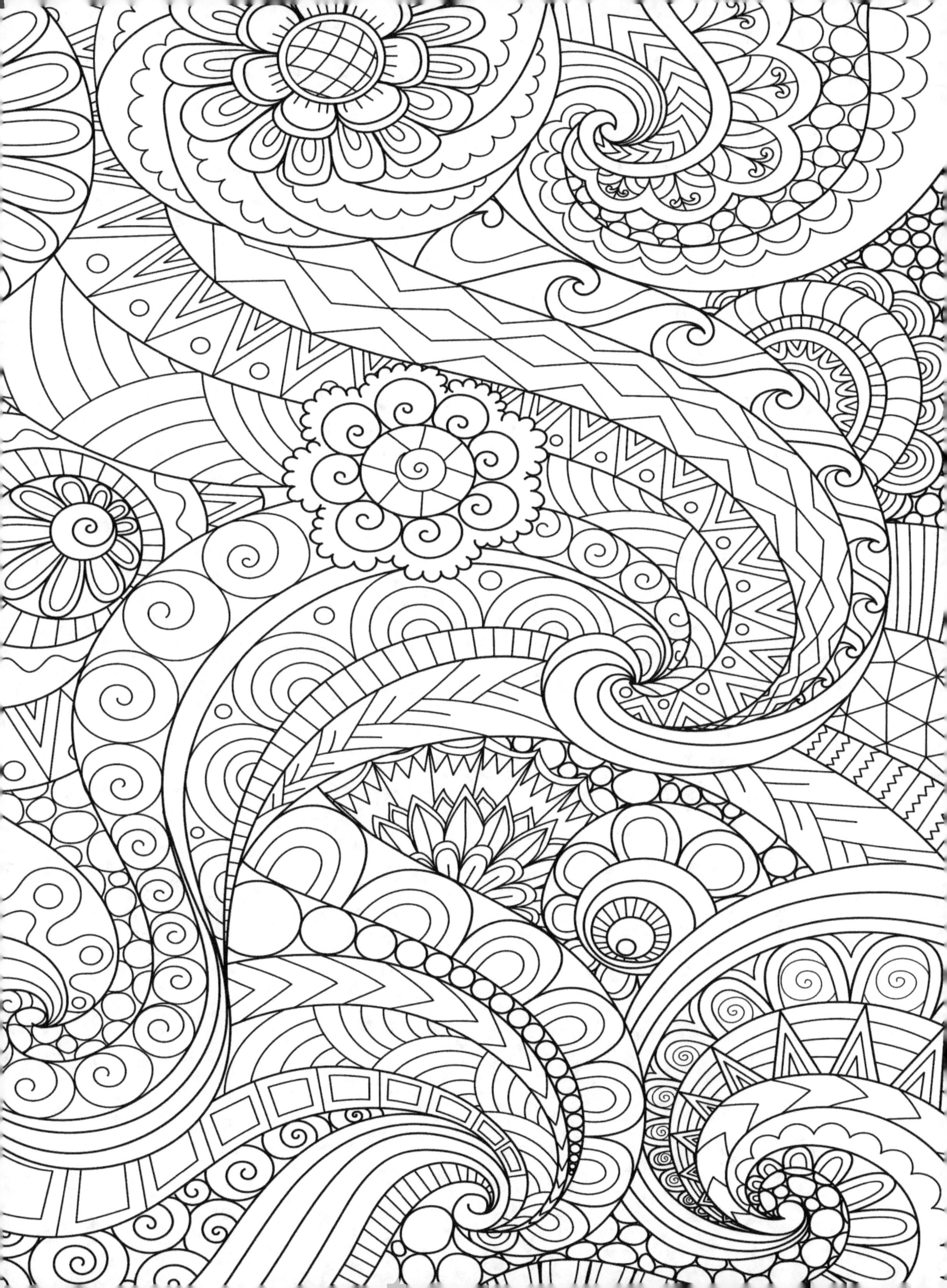

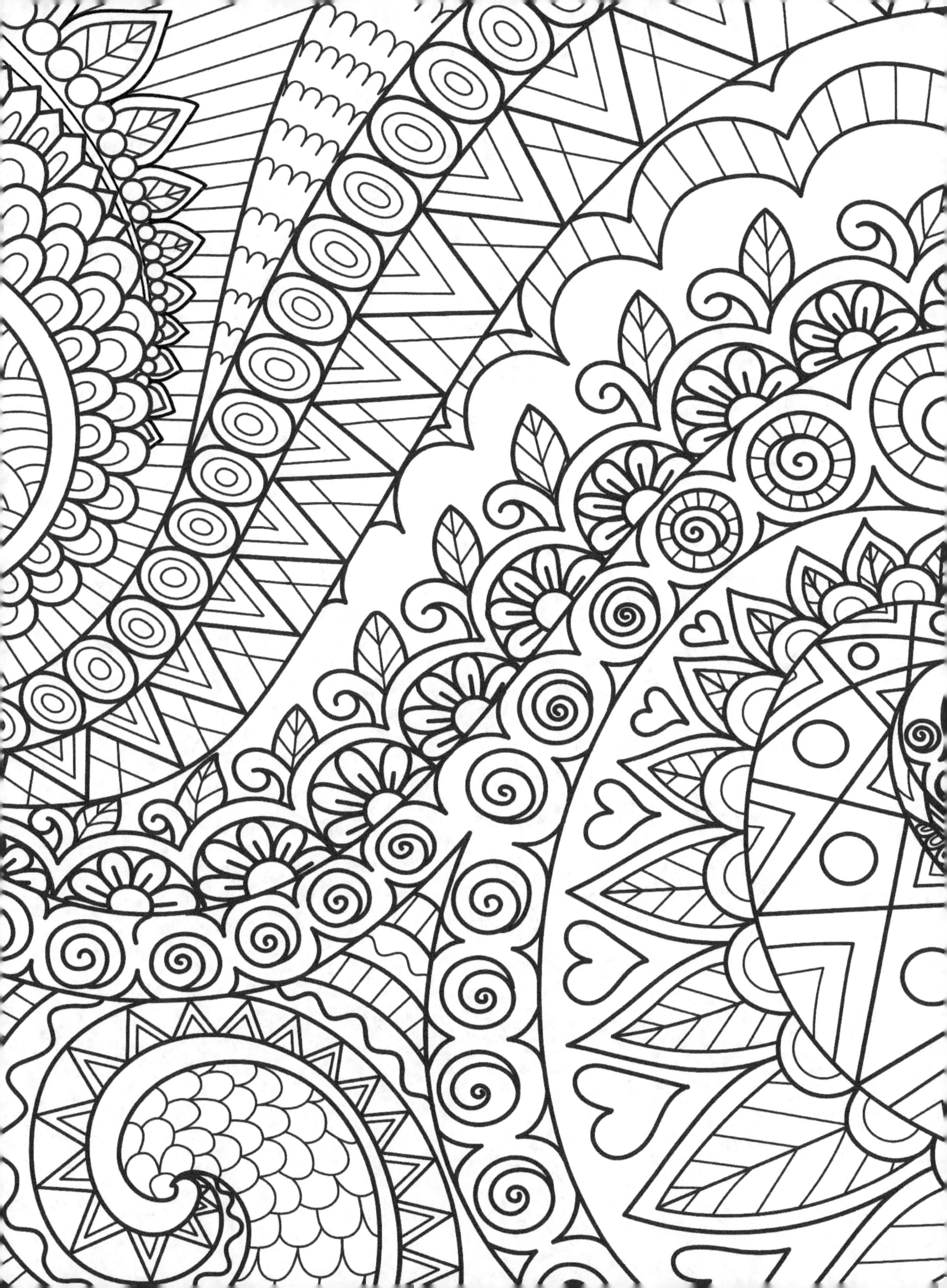

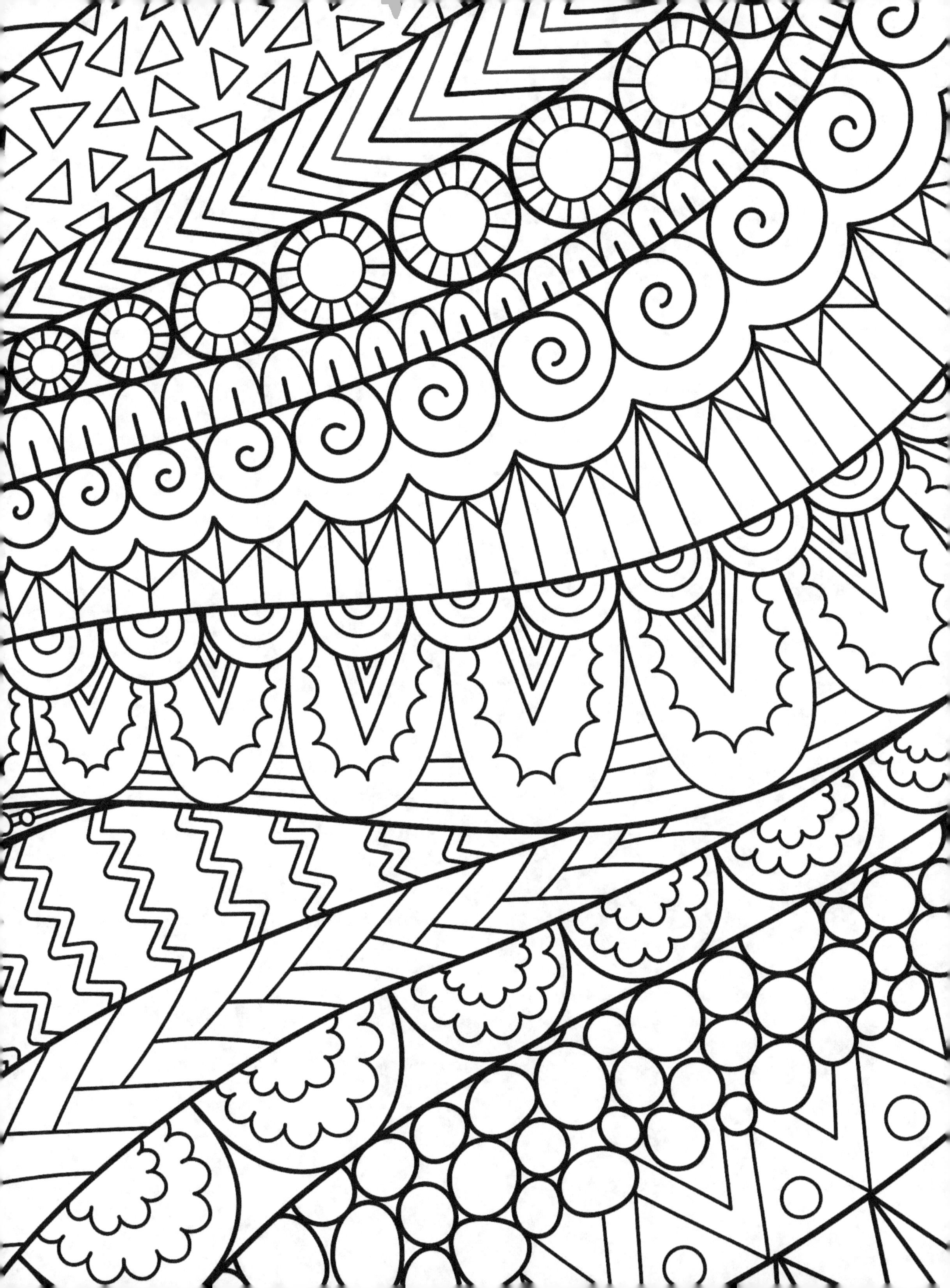

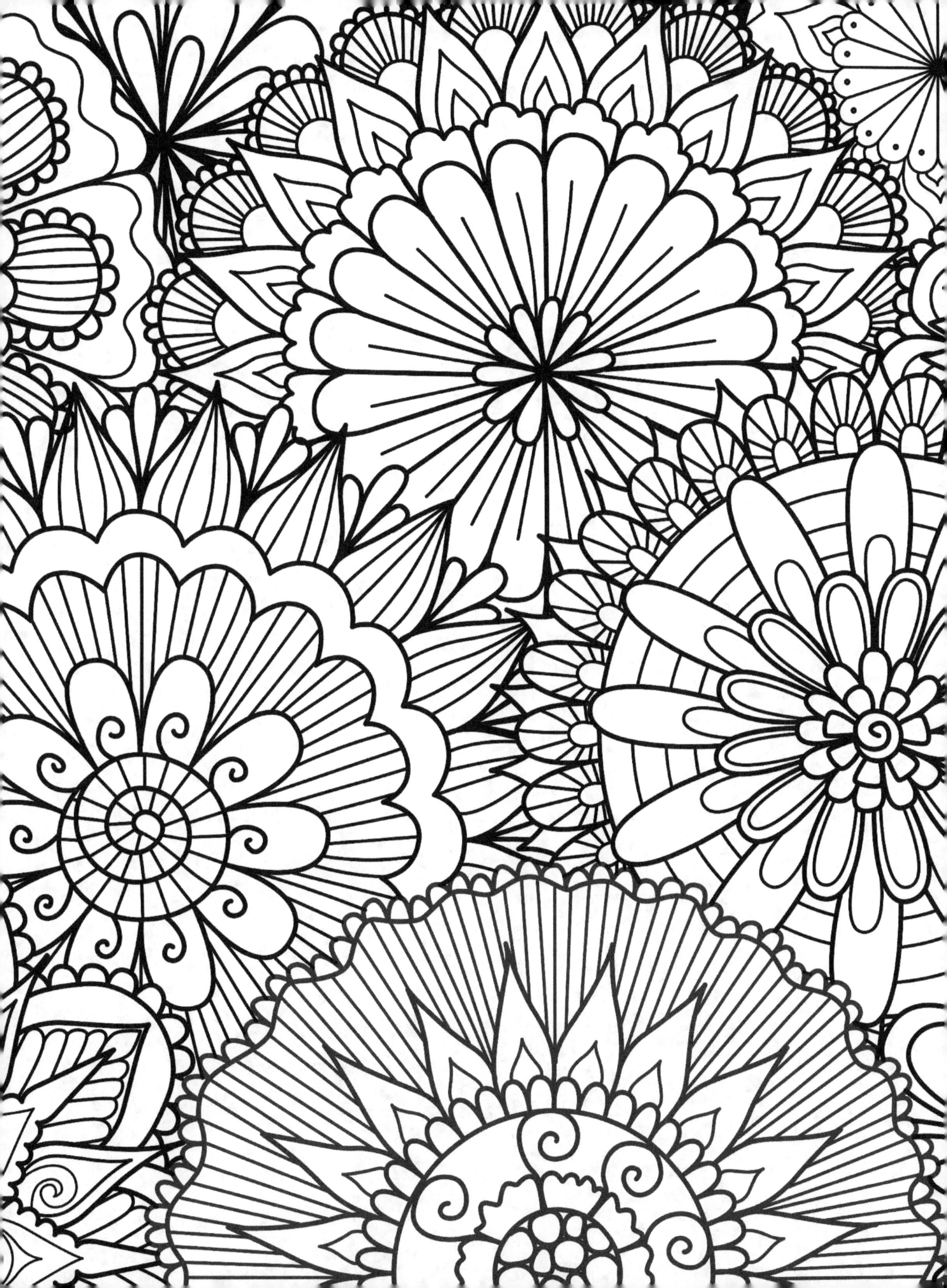

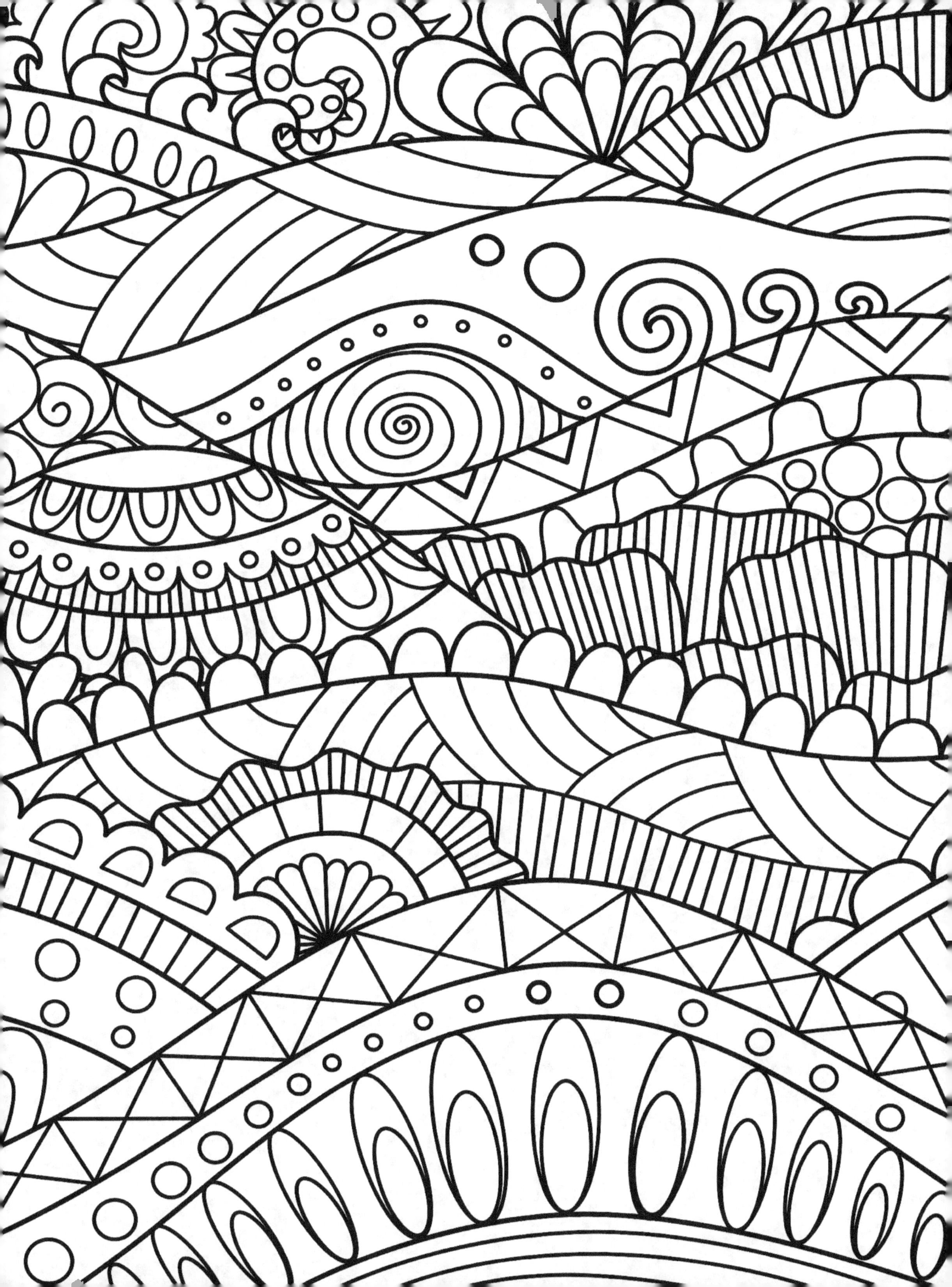

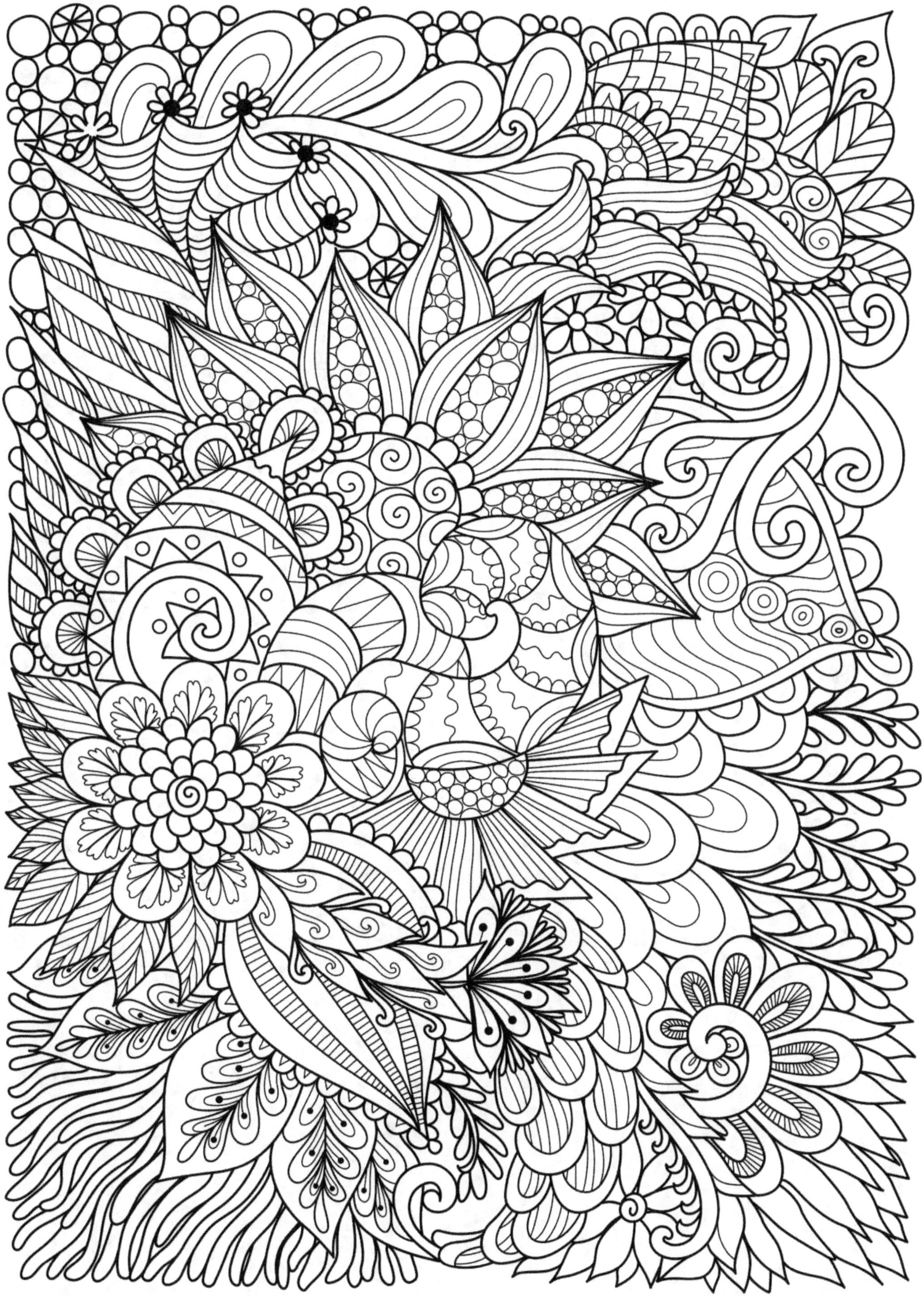

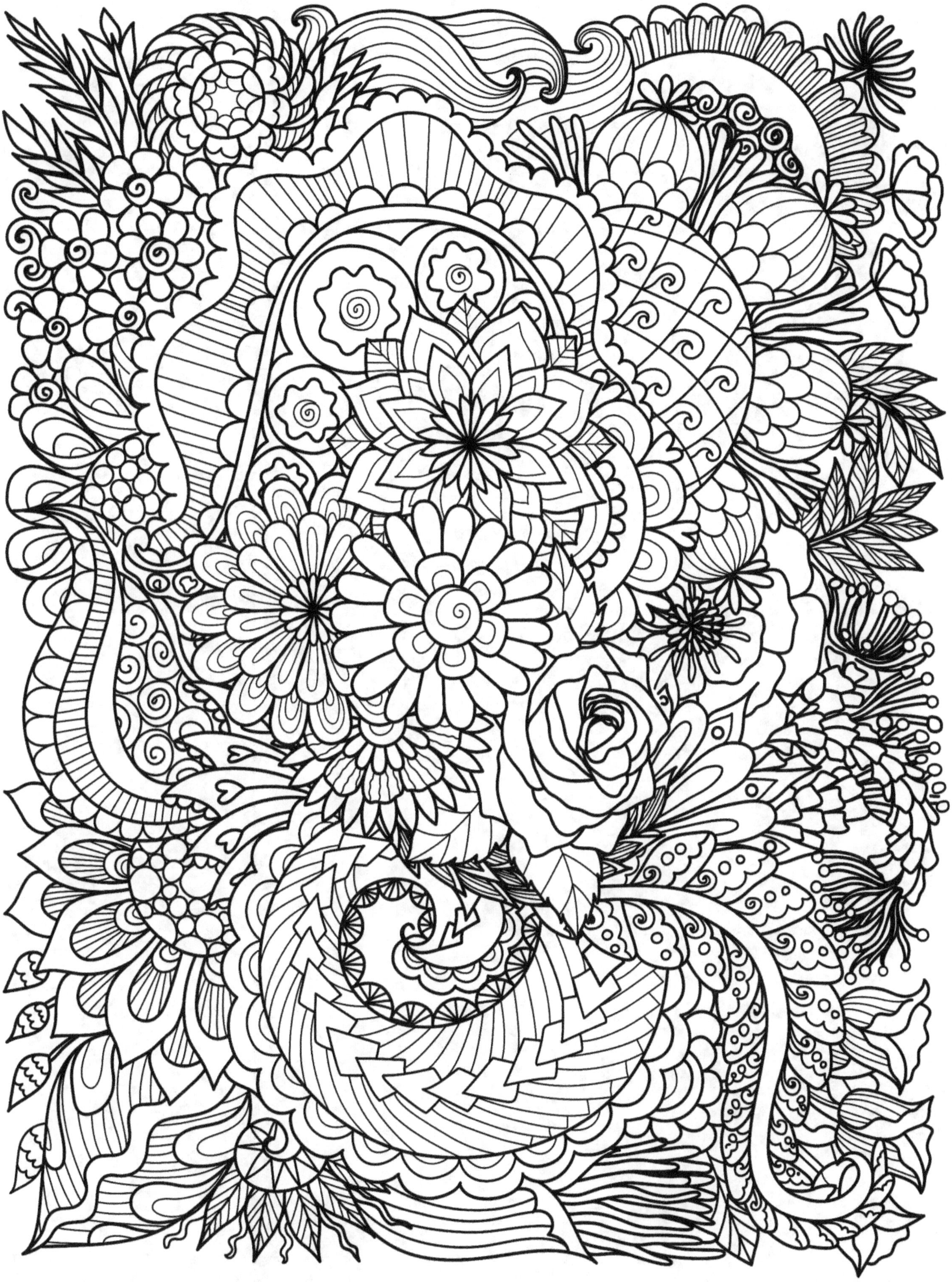

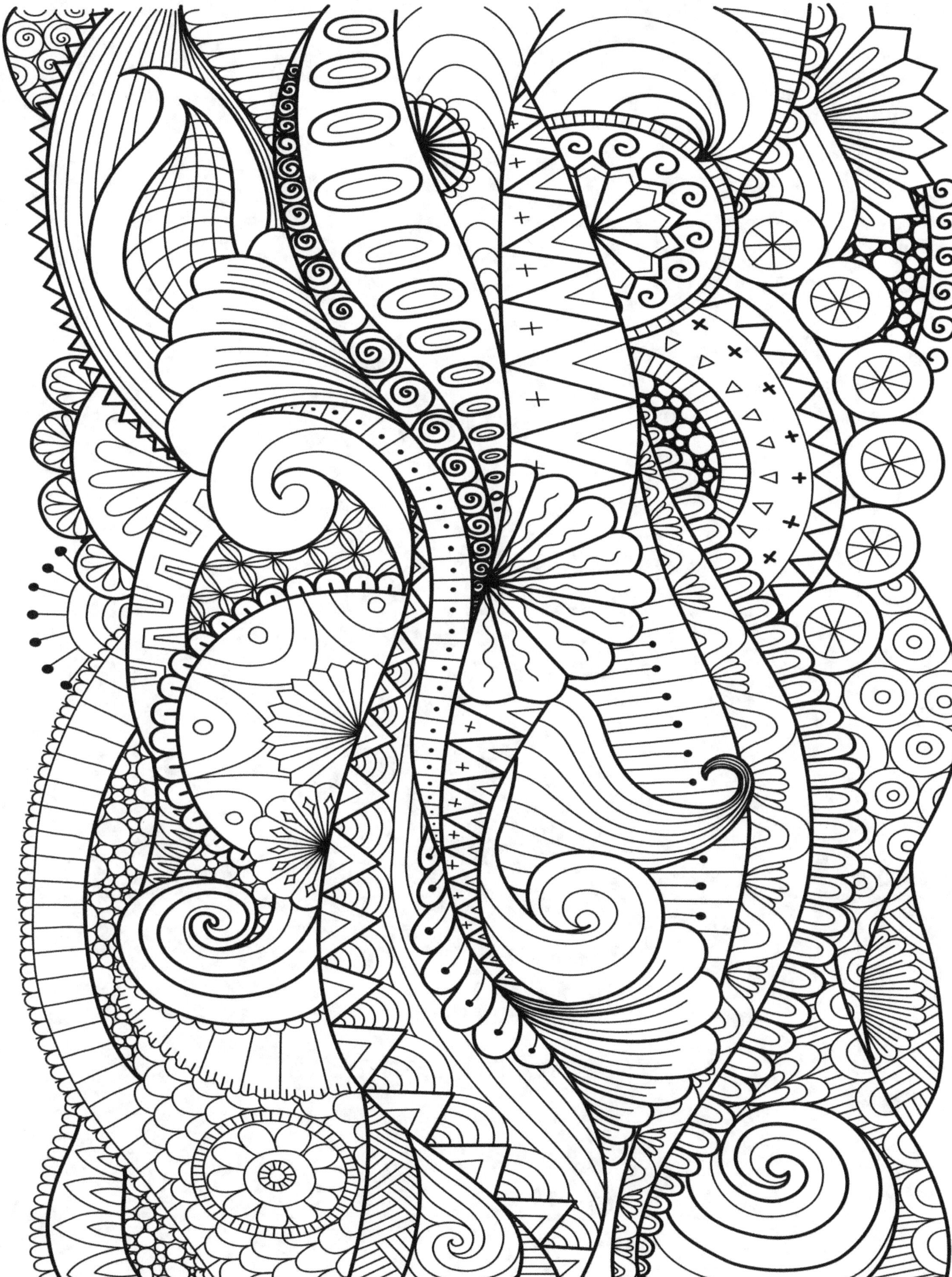

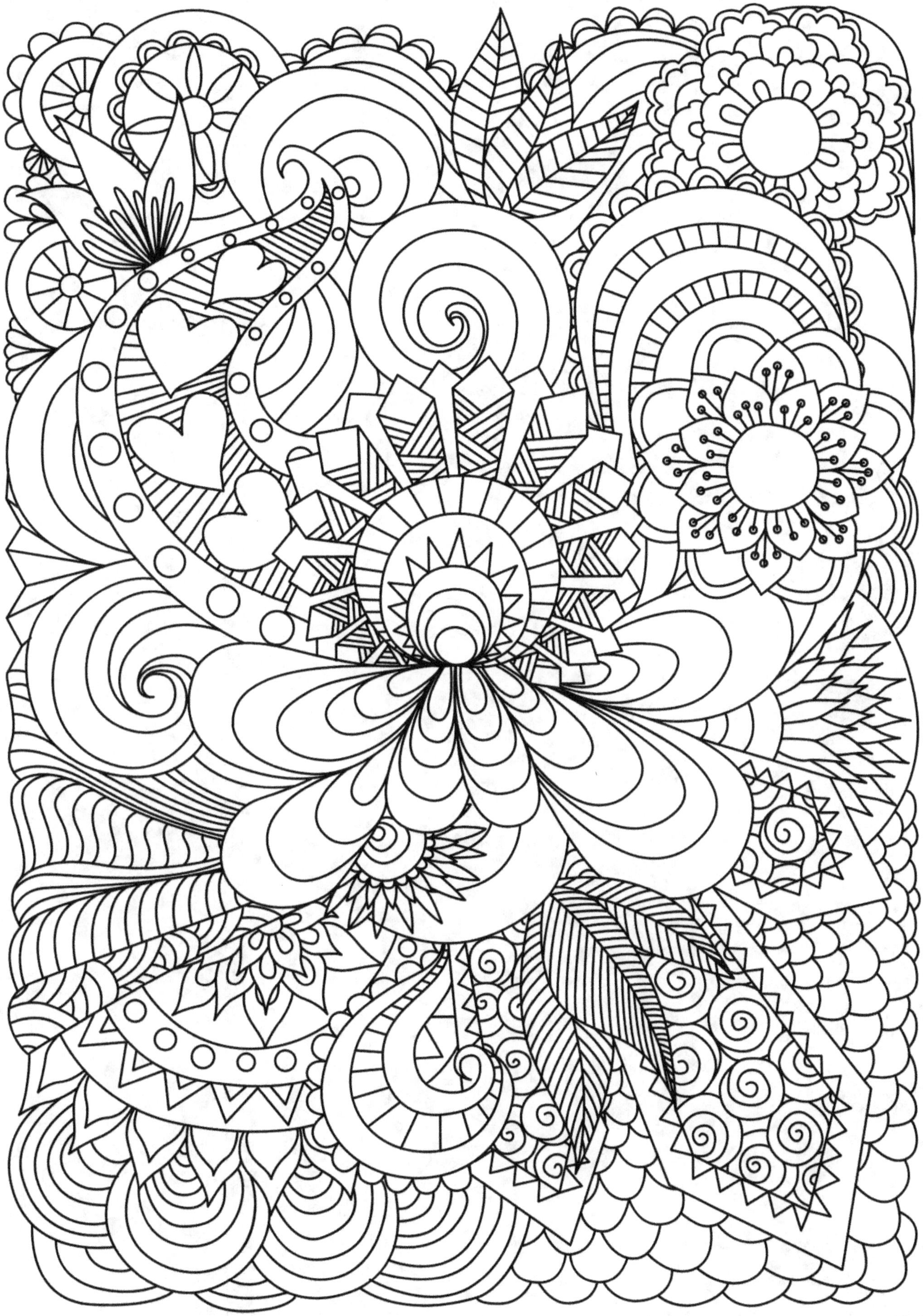

www.ingramcontent.com/pod-product-compliance
Lightning Source LLC
Chambersburg PA
CBHW081539220526
45467CB00010B/3259
9798715476302